Sharks

Therese Shea

New York

Published in 2007 by The Rosen Publishing Group, Inc.
29 East 21st Street, New York, NY 10010

Book Design: Daniel Hosek

Photo Credits: Cover © Boyd McGregor/Getty Images; p. 5 © SeaChange Technology/Getty Images; pp. 7, 11 © Keir Davis/Shutterstock; pp. 9, 19, 22 © Ian Scott/Shutterstock; p. 13 © Photodisc; p. 15 © wheatley/Shutterstock; p. 17 © Justin Sullivan/Getty Images; p. 21 © Hotli Simanjuntak/AFP/Getty Images.

Library of Congress Cataloging-in-Publication Data

Shea, Therese.
Sharks / Therese Shea.
p. cm. -- (Big bad biters)
Includes bibliographical references and index.
ISBN-13: 978-1-4042-3519-9
ISBN-10: 1-4042-3519-1
1. Sharks--Juvenile literature. I. Title. II. Series: Shea. Therese. Big bad biters.
QL638.9.S524 2007
597.3--dc22
2006014645

Manufactured in the United States of America

Contents

Sharks: Scary or Cool?

Do you think sharks are scary? They have so many teeth! Maybe you have seen them attack people in movies. In real life, sharks don't hurt people very often. They mostly use their teeth to eat fish.

Sharks have been on this planet since long before dinosaurs walked Earth. They are some of the best hunters in the ocean. Some are very fast swimmers, too. Let's learn more cool facts about sharks!

Some sharks can jump 20 feet (6.1 m) above the water.

A Different Kind of Fish

Did you know that sharks are fish? Like all fish, they live in water and breathe through **gills**. Unlike other fish, sharks don't have bones. Their bodies are shaped by **cartilage**, which is hard and bendable. You have cartilage at the end of your nose.

Sharks have many rows of teeth. Some sharks have thousands of teeth! A tooth may last only a week in a shark's mouth. When a shark loses a tooth, a new one moves into its place.

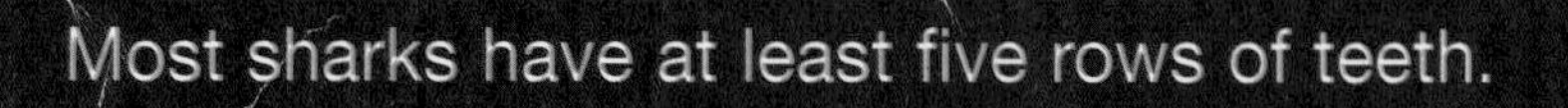

Most sharks have at least five rows of teeth.

All Kinds of Sharks

There are over 350 kinds of sharks all over the world. They have many shapes, colors, and sizes. The biggest sharks are called whale sharks. They can be up to 60 feet (18.3 m) long! The smallest sharks are called dwarf lanternfish. Some are only 6 inches (15.2 cm) long.

Most sharks have rounded bodies that allow them to swim quickly through the water. Some sharks have flat bodies that help them move along the ocean floor.

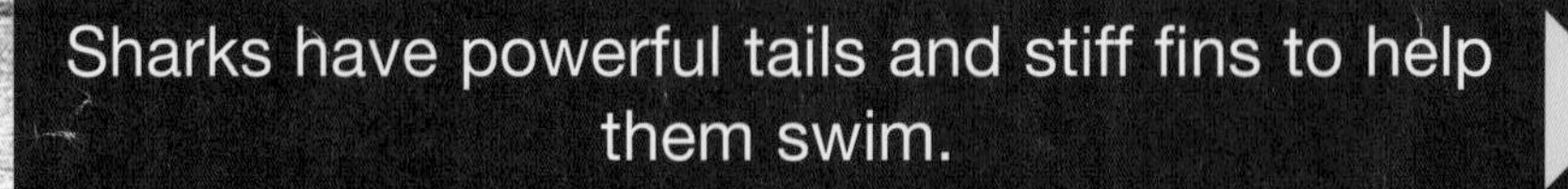

Sharks have powerful tails and stiff fins to help them swim.

Do Sharks Breathe?

Sharks need **oxygen** to live—just like we do! However, they don't breathe air. Many sharks swim to get oxygen. When they swim, water flows into their mouths. It passes over their gills. The gills take oxygen from the water. Then the water goes out the gill openings.

Some sharks at the bottom of the ocean don't need to swim for oxygen. They have **muscles** in their mouths that pump water over their gills.

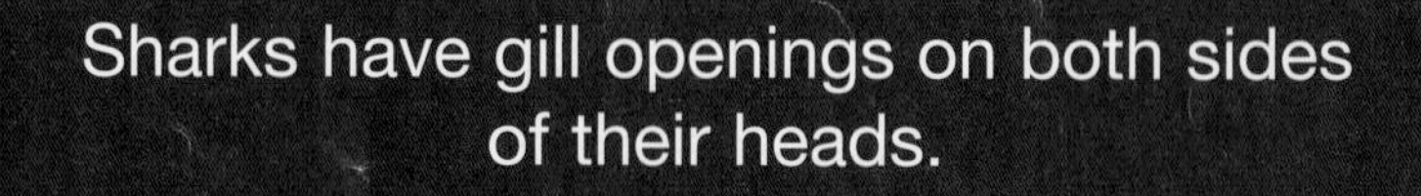
Sharks have gill openings on both sides of their heads.

Where Do Sharks Live?

Some sharks live in cold, deep parts of the ocean. Others live in warm waters by the coast. Sharks can also be found in rivers and lakes near the ocean. Sharks usually live in salt water. However, one kind of shark has even been found in freshwater lakes.

Some sharks, like hammerheads, **migrate**. They stay in one place in the summer and move to another place in the winter. They like to be in warm water.

Hammerheads can be found all over the world.

Time to Eat!

Sharks are **predators**. This means they hunt other animals. Sharks use their teeth to attack their **prey**. Sharks with narrow, sharp teeth eat animals such as small sharks and whales, fish, squid, seals, and sea lions. Sharks with thick, flat teeth eat crabs and other animals with hard shells.

You may think sharks are always hungry and looking for food. That's not true. Some sharks eat only one small meal every 2 or 3 days.

Basking sharks can be up to 40 feet (12.2 m) long. They eat very small fish and fish eggs.

Shark Pups

Most female sharks don't lay eggs like other fish. Some keep their eggs inside their bodies until they hatch. Others give birth to live babies, or **pups**. However, sharks that live near the ocean floor may lay eggs. They have more pups than other kinds of sharks.

A female shark has pups once a year. Some have sixty or more pups at a time. Others may have only two pups at a time.

Shark pups, like this white-tipped shark, must care for themselves right after they are born.

Finding Food

Did you know that sharks hear well? They can hear very low sounds, like prey moving through the water. Some sharks can also see in dark places. They can even see some colors.

Sharks also have a special way of finding food. They have special tubes in their heads. These tubes help them to sense **electricity** that comes from fish gills. They may also be able to sense the direction the electricity comes from.

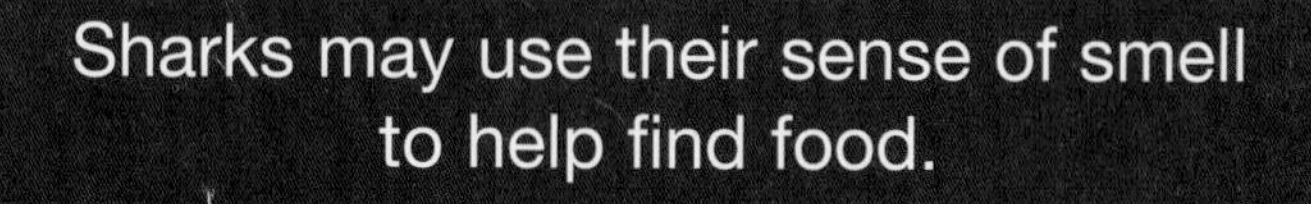
Sharks may use their sense of smell to help find food.

Shark Enemies

Sharks are powerful and scary. Do they have enemies in the ocean? Yes, they do! They are their own enemies. Large sharks eat smaller sharks.

Sharks have a worse enemy on land. People hunt sharks. They eat shark meat, use sharkskin for clothing, and make jewelry with shark teeth. Shark fin soup is popular in some places. One bowl can cost more than $300! Some kinds of sharks were hunted so much in the past that they almost disappeared.

Laws had to be passed to stop shark hunters.

Do We Need Sharks?

Do we need sharks? Yes! Sharks eat ocean animals. Without sharks, there might be too many of some ocean animals. These animals could eat too many ocean plants. This would cause other ocean animals to die. Sharks help keep the ocean a healthy place for fish, plants, and people, too!

Glossary

cartilage (KAR-tuh-lihj) A bendable matter that gives shape to some animal bodies.

electricity (ih-lehk-TRIH-suh-tee) A type of power.

gill (GIHL) A part of a fish that gets oxygen from the water.

migrate (MY-grayt) When large groups of animals move from one place to another.

muscle (MUH-suhl) A part of a body that is connected to bones and helps them move.

oxygen (AHK-sih-juhn) A gas needed for life.

predator (PREH-duh-tuhr) An animal that hunts other animals as food.

prey (PRAY) An animal that is hunted by another animal as food.

pup (PUHP) The name for some kinds of baby animals.

Index

Web Sites

Due to the changing nature of Internet links, PowerKids Press has developed an online list of Web sites related to the subject of this book. This site is updated regularly. Please use this link to access the list:
http://www.powerkidslinks.com/biters/sharks/

CENTRAL ISLIP PUBLIC LIBRARY
3 1800 00238 7526